Messages *from the* Shore

by Victor B. Scheffer

Pacific Search Press/nature

Pacific Search Press, 715 Harrison Street, Seattle, Washington 98109
©1976, 1977 by Pacific Search Press. All rights reserved
This book first appeared in *Pacific Search* magazine in a different form
Printed in the United States of America
Designed by Lou Rivera
Photographs by Victor B. Scheffer
Cover photo: Bodelteh Islets in sunset, as seen from Cape Alava, Washington

Library of Congress Cataloging in Publication Data
Scheffer, Victor B
Messages from the shore.
1. Seashore biology.   1. Title.
QH95.7.S3   574.909'4'6   77-78280
ISBN 0-914718-24-X pbk.

Contents

Beauty and Meaning

Renewal . . . renewal . . . renewal . . . is the message of the waves

Cockle, Clinocardium nuttalli, *Whidbey Island, Washington*

Some years ago I lived at the edge of a tropical sea where the native people in all innocence would dispose of empty rum bottles, coconut husks, conch shells, broken furniture, dolls without heads, and fish bones by dumping them on the white coral beaches. There the waves would eventually crush the debris, and the hot sun would purify the fragments. The custom was all very practical, I suppose, yet it cut deeply into my spirit, for I had been raised from boyhood to think of the seashores everywhere as special and wonderful places.

The edge of the sea has a pull that draws poets, artists, and young lovers — those who live in imaginary worlds. It has other qualities that draw naturalists — those who study the real world in its infinite manifestations. It has two strong messages — its beauty and its meaning. Certain patterns along the shore provoke pure emotion, while others help us appreciate the materials and the forces of our planet, and the never-ending play between them. Our intuitive feeling for the shore and our knowledge of its structure seem after a while to blend in our thoughts; we develop a lifelong conservation ethic toward this meeting place between earth and water.

There is, I think, a fundamental attraction of the shore that is generated by *time* — by duration without apparent end or beginning. We feel this quality when we stand quietly on a beach and open our senses to all of its inflooding sounds, images, and odors. It is a subtle quality, expressed in some bit of driftwood come to final rest, or in a fragment of a lost ship half-buried in the sand, or in a primeval tune carried by the wind. We are led to imagine that the tune will have no finale, and in the thought we are encouraged to go on with the living of our own daily lives.

Another basic attraction of the shore is its cleanliness. No other place on earth, no other ecosystem, is cleansed as often by wind and water and patrolled as often by scavengers, or litter-pickers. From the time of its genesis nearly five billion years ago, the margin of the World Ocean has never for a moment been still. The tidal pull of heavenly bodies, especially of the moon and the sun, allows the sea no rest.

Beachcombers, Iron Springs, Washington

Detail of rocks on tidal beach, Whidbey Island, Washington

8

Through day and night the scavengers are busy. The bacteria and the nameless crawlers neither plant nor animal; the rotifers and mudworms of a thousand shapes and colors; starfishes and urchins; snails, crabs, and fishes — all are prowling the shallows in search of food. On the beaches above the sea — gulls, crows, and ravens; skunks, weasels, otters, raccoons, bears, coyotes, and foxes are hunting for edible remains swept ashore by the waves. The scavengers reduce organic masses to molecules. Even the looming carcass of a whale is reduced in time to particles that ultimately become the building blocks of new lives.

In order of abundance: tower shells (Turitella), *cockles* (Trachycardium),
olives (Oliva), *and worm shells* (Serpulorbis), *Sea of Cortez, Mexico*

The sea is the great recycler. It composes and decomposes and
recomposes. Renewal . . . renewal . . . renewal . . . is the message of
the waves.

Carved by Water and Wind

Water, wind, and drifting sand grains produce a soft geometry

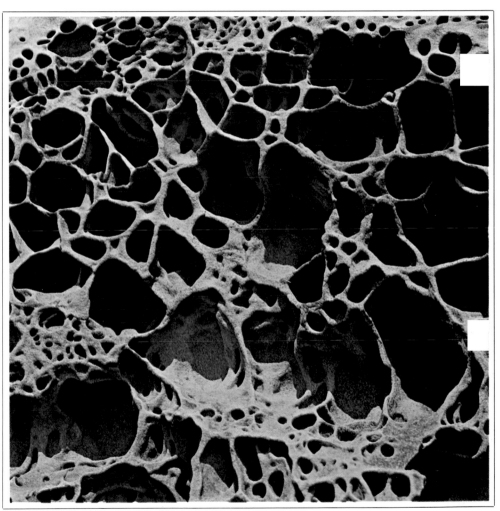

Sandstone "honeycomb," Skagit County, Washington

From the idea that all things in the universe, including patterns of the shore, are "created" it is only a short jump to the idea that Nature is a creative artist in her own right. Here the true artist will demur. Natural compositions, he or she will say, are only art sources, or inspirations. But surely no harm is done, and some pleasure is gained, by humanizing those lifeless agents that operate along the shore and are endlessly busy at carving, scouring, etching, and polishing rocks, driftwood, and the bones and shells of sea creatures. The end products often look as though they have been crafted by human hands. Water, wind, and drifting sand grains can produce a soft geometry, or balance, or fundamental rightness that instantly strikes us as "artistic."

A spruce tree, fallen from a streamside in the forest, may float to shore, be cruelly pounded year after year by winter storms, and be reduced finally to a stubborn mass of roots still clutching the boulders that it seized from the earth while it was growing. Here the shapes and textures of the dissected wood lead one to suppose that Nature, like a human artist, is forever trying to improve her techniques and to seek new ways of expressing her truths. "Found art" on the beach often has this quality that implies care and patience in its creation.

Sculpture on the shore is independent of scale; carvings of microscopic size can be found beside colossal statues of native rock. I sometimes kneel in the sand and look through a hand lens at the glancing colors of tiny agates, or the clean lines where the scoured ribs of a herring join the backbone, or the wide variety of plumes on the shaft of a gull feather.

Nearly always the carved things of the shore have a textural dimension. They make us want to stroke them or turn them over in our hands.

In the clay stone cliffs along many of Washington State's Puget Sound beaches (Point Defiance, Hood Head, and Holmes Harbor among them), you can find concretions that look at first glance like artifacts. Smooth and softly rounded, they resemble balls, dolls, animals, faces, or what-you-will. They are, so to speak, sculptures in reverse. They are formed when silica or lime in solution cements particles of clay, starting

Sitka spruce with rocks seized by growing roots, Olympic seacoast, Washington

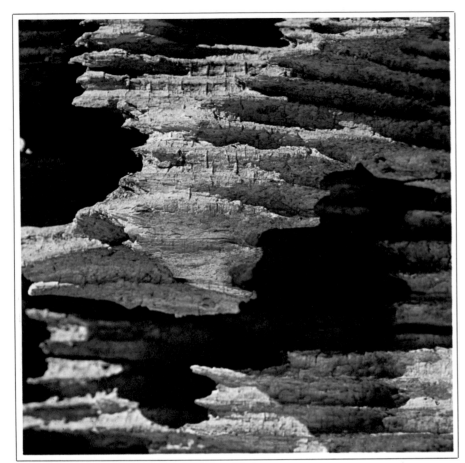

Douglas fir driftwood sculptured by the sea, Washington coast

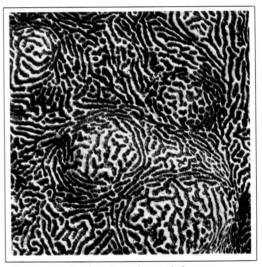

*Brain coral (Diploria), nonliving skeletons
cemented in bedrock of beach,
Grand Cayman Island, British West Indies*

from an inner nucleus — such as an embedded fragment of shell —
and slowly working outward in all directions. Erosion finally exposes
the concretions, and being harder than the matrix in which they grew,
they tumble to the beach intact. The end products look like works that
an artist might have made by sandblasting large, irregular lumps of
clay stone.

Coarse grains of sand, agate or similar, Yachats, Oregon

Sorted Patterns *Fabrics and tapestries*

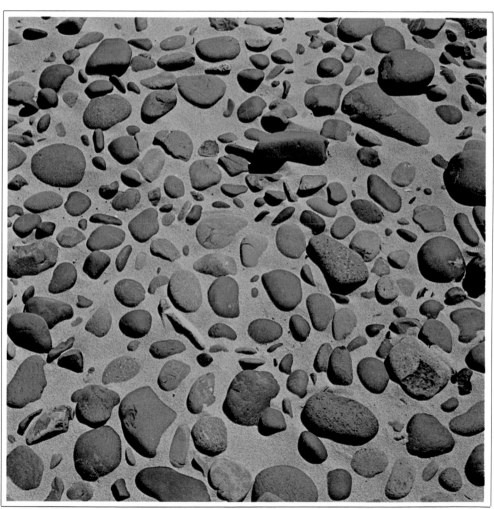

Seashore rocks partly buried in summer sand, Newport, Oregon

Storm-cast logs on Beverly Beach,
Whidbey Island, Washington

The never-ending reactions of forces and materials at the shore create an infinite variety of sorted patterns. These are fabrics woven by a classifying process in which water and wind feel and identify the size, weight, and shape of sand grains, pebbles, bits of wood, seaweed, shells, feathers, and foam. Beachcombers and rock hounds soon learn to identify certain windrows on the beach as promising to be richer than others.

Made without effort, and often in the span of moments, sorted patterns are peculiarly natural; seldom can they be matched by human artifice. They have an inherent freedom that artists and engineers can appreciate but cannot easily imitate. Some years ago, when I first began to photograph seashore animals, I would often take a specimen into my laboratory and pose it on a background of sand nicely smoothed by a trowel. Unfortunately, on the finished photograph the background would come out looking as though it had been nicely smoothed by a trowel!

Wave-rippled sand, Netarts seashore, Oregon

After we begin to look carefully at the "simple" tapestries of the shore, we begin to see their real complexity and to speculate with growing wonder on their origins. Many contain the rhythms of waves; their plans are repetitive. Many show in structure the results of moving forces of varying power — here perhaps a swift current that laid down a warp of driftwood, there a gentle current that interlaced a woof of sea grasses.

Shell-fragment beach, Hackney Island, Washington

Off the east coast of Whidbey Island, Washington, there is an islet, less than an acre in size, known locally as Baby Island (though on the charts as Hackney Island). It is connected to Whidbey by a sandspit, which is bare at ebb tide. The spit is shining white and can be seen from a distance of several miles. Drawn by curiosity, I once landed on it and found that it is covered with broken bits of white shells cast up by the eddying currents. Mussels, butter clams, cockles, barnacles, limpets, whelks, and other common shellfish — all are represented here in this little mollusk cemetery. The shells are spatially sorted by species and by differences in structure.

The message in a pile of drift-logs lying far above the tide line strikes clearly when we try to imagine the fury of that certain onshore wind, coupled with a rising tide, that must have carried the many-ton timbers to their resting place. Some of them, far-gone in decay and riddled with

Natural arrangement of rocks and driftwood, Olympic seacoast, Washington

the roots of plants, were doubtless cast up before the time of anyone now living. Meteorologists speak of statistical storms, or the events that are likely to occur once a year, or a century, or a millennium. The longer the time interval, the greater the probability of a catastrophic event. These events, many of which leave lasting scars on the landscape, are often freak combinations involving a hurricane, a great tide, a cloudburst, or an earthquake.

Fantasy and Illusion *Playing an intricate game with Nature*

Rain-wet rocks on seashore, Agate Beach, Oregon

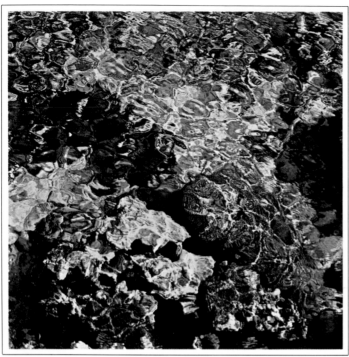

Shallow tide pool, Grand Cayman Island, British West Indies

Each of us is a divided self, acting in both real and imaginary worlds. Most of us, when we stay for a while on an ocean beach and try to lose ourselves among its images, can slip easily from one world into the other. We gain extrasensory perception. Mirrors and black shadows in the wetness of rocks become rooms populated by goblins. Tide pool galleries alive with light and motion become fairy places. At our feet, small clearings of sand, dimpled by the feet of crabs, become lunar landscapes crossed by the tracks of vehicles. Faint, faraway islands become beasts in a row, their backs above the sea, their rough tails blurring on the rim of the sky.

One of the quicker ways to enter a seashore realm of fantasy and illusion is to trail behind a boy or girl about five years old. Children delight in being scared by crocodiles and monsters where we adults see only driftwood and tangled kelp. In having learned facts about matter

25

Beachcombers and nature students at low tide, Seal Rock State Park, Oregon

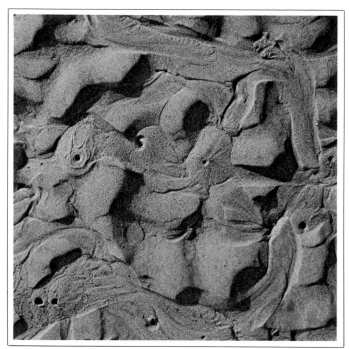

Sand patterns with craters burrowed by ghost prawns,
Netarts seashore, Oregon

and substance, we have lost the ability to see things that children find so plainly illuminated. For us, a walk on the beach is too often purposeful. Not to say that the children wander aimlessly; they are busy playing an intricate game with Nature.

Years ago when I lived on a coral island, I spent delightful hours hiking along the intertidal zone, looking for odd forms of branching corals. These shallow-water animals (*Porites*) are treelike in shape and stony in structure. They are often torn loose from their moorings by storms and are cast upon the shore, where they fade to a soft, eggshell white. I found fragments that seemed to be bodies joined in dance — their arms and legs poised in graceful curves. Or again, they may be numbers and letters in some unearthly language, spelling out the message of organic diversity.

Above the level of the molecule, no two things in the universe are alike.

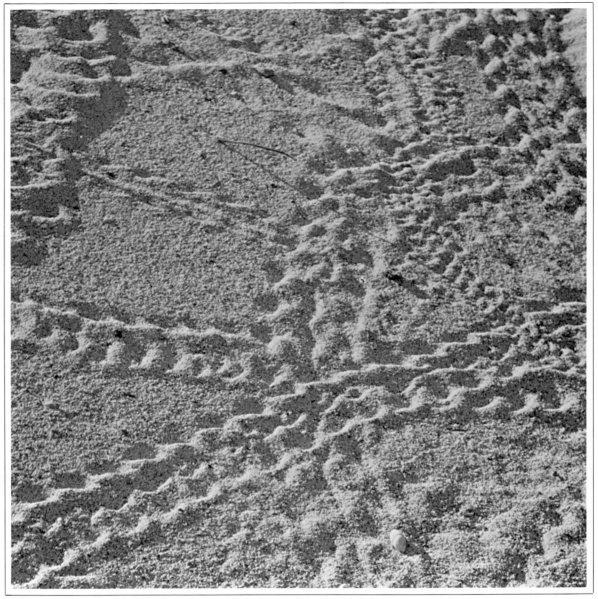

"A busy night at Crab Crossing" — *tracks in sand, ghost crabs and land crabs,*
Grand Cayman Island, British West Indies

Sea and Land in Contest *An arena where lifeless and living materials confront one another endlessly*

Surf at South Point, Island of Hawaii

The shores of the World Ocean are records of conflict, competition, and perpetual change. The tidal zone, more so than any other place on earth, is an arena where lifeless and living materials confront one another endlessly, spend and regain their energies, and form and reform their shapes.

When a great sea comber slams against a cliff, liquid water with the power of dynamite meets solid rock. The motion is largely wasted in heat and sound, but in some tiny crevice a few drops of water are left behind. There they seize the right moment to exert hydraulic pressure — and down comes a flake of rock. The contest is not one-sided. As each flake falls to the sea, it is carried by currents to quiet bays, where it is dropped. Here the flakes accumulate as sandbars and, in the course of time, are knit together by the roots of salt grasses, shrubs, and trees. The shore reclaims a transitory victory over the sea.

I used to travel by ship every spring to the Bering Sea, past the lighthouse tower that rose ninety-two feet above the water at Scotch Cap on Unimak Island. In 1946 the light had disappeared. A great wave, born in the convulsions of an Aleutian earthquake, had risen silently on the night of April first and swept away the steel and concrete tower, along with the five men who maintained it.

As the ocean rolls through geologic time, it leaves myriad clues to its long history. Some of them are the petrified bodies, or the delicate imprints or casts, of organisms that died in the sea and whose traces were eventually exposed when marine sediments were lifted into daylight by warping of the earth's crust. Even the last little wave that lapped on a sandy beach on a quiet morning in the Triassic may have left its testimony, to be read by men two hundred million years later when a slab of rippled sandstone falls from a cliff above the shore.

On a flat muddy beach, you often see where tensions between solid and liquid have been resolved in patterns almost as regular as computer print-outs. As a result of many-directional stresses, little islands of dried mud become separated by deep cracks. The patterns tell of arrested motion — of armistice, or compromise between forces.

Pacific surf creaming on Point Grenville, Washington

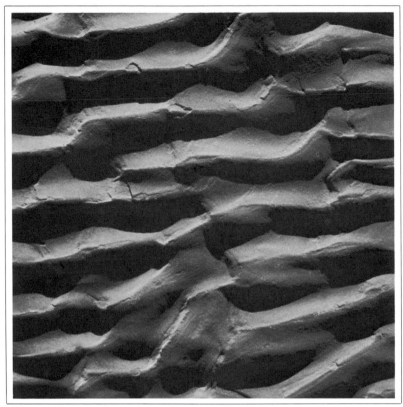

*Wave marks in sandstone, Lykins Formation (Permo-Triassic),
Fort Collins, Colorado*

Patterns of conflict between sea and land are often sharply displayed in tidal basins that are protected from the open sea, such as Grays Harbor, Washington. At low tide on the mudflats you can see (especially from an airplane) numberless veins and venules, which indicate the changing power and direction of ebbing currents. Tomorrow, and in all tomorrows, the designs will be subtly different.

Crack pattern in drying mud, lagoon near Conch Point, Grand Cayman Island, British West Indies

33

Origins and Evolution

The edge of the sea offers an abbreviated history of all life

"Fossils of the future?" — *waveworn fragments of conch shells,*
Grand Cayman Island, British West Indies

West Indian starfish, Oreaster reticulatus, *Grand Cayman Island, British West Indies*

Life on earth began in the Precambrian seas thirty million centuries ago, in particles that were little more than chemical bits having the power to grow and to subdivide themselves. The nourishing amniotic tides of the ancient seas were fresher and warmer than those of today, and they moved beneath a suffocating atmosphere that held only traces of oxygen. Perhaps (though we shall never know), for a microsecond of time, there was only one living thing. Much later, complex organisms evolved from the unicellular bits, and some of them gradually oozed or crawled along separate pathways, through quiet estuaries and coastal swamps, onto the land.

Twenty-rayed starfish, Pycnopodia helianthoides, *Point of Arches, Washington*

Sand dollar, Dendraster excentricus, *an echinoderm; dead individual from which spines have eroded, Puget Sound, Washington*

38

Today the edge of the sea offers an abbreviated history of all life. Old organisms and new, first families and late arrivals, conservatives and progressives jostle here for existence. Some living marine worms, sponges, and jellyfishes are look-alikes of ancestors whose remains lie in rocks a half-billion years old. In contrast, the sea otter of the North Pacific ventured into the ocean only yesterday, some two million years ago.

Green sea anemone, Anthopleura xanthogrammica, *Olympic seacoast, Washington*

Four groups of animals with modern descendants remain locked in the salty sea. They are the echinoderms (starfishes, sea urchins, sea cucumbers, and feather stars), the lamp shells, the arrow worms, and the comb jellies. For reasons unknown, these creatures of ancient lineage have never been able to pioneer the land or its fresh waters.

While continents were drifting, while polar ice was advancing or retreating, while volcanoes were darkening the skies or were sleeping, and while sea levels were rising or falling, the long curving shorelines remained. They stood as frontiers, or testing grounds, which ancestral plants and animals were forever trying to cross, at first from the sea to the land and later in both directions.

About 1.5 million species of living organisms are known, of which at least 100,000 inhabit marine shores and shallows. Many a naturalist, impressed by the extravagance of life along the shore, thinks of Darwinian fitness and "natural selection." Before Darwin, philosopher Herbert Spencer had introduced the phrase "survival of the fittest." The living zoologist L. Harrison Matthews proposes "natural rejection." So, while the naturalist is enjoying the vital richness at his feet, he is also thinking of organic function, adaptation, and response. He knows that throughout time, all changes in body form and behavior of organisms are surely directed toward the evolution of sensible shapes and practical ways of life.

Yet no plant or animal knows the meaning of progress; none has a goal or a sense of direction. For each, the momentary problems of living are met with momentary solutions.

Eroded tests of sea urchins (Diadema *and* Lytechinus) *on beach of Grand Cayman Island, British West Indies*

The Seaweeds: Marine Pioneers
Successful in their own slippery ways

Marine algae (mainly Fucus *and* Ulva*), Whidbey Island, Washington*

T he poet Shelley called them "the oozy woods which wear / The sapless foliage of the ocean." The seaweeds, or marine algae, have a history that stems from the Precambrian, a billion years ago. Successful in their own slippery ways, they now number more than five thousand species and live in all the marine shallows of the world. Daily beset by changes in temperature, salinity, winds, and currents, they endure. The common rockweed *(Fucus)* of our North American shores can survive for hours in a cold, pounding surf and then, when the tide falls, survive for hours under a blistering sun.

Some seaweeds have the shapes of ribbons; others, of lace, feathers, threads, whips, fans, or seamless webs. One, known as deadman's fingers, is a cluster of thin, fluid-filled sacs. Surely the great variety of shapes is an indication that these plants fill many separate, peculiar ecologic niches, though the true nature of the niches is still largely unknown.

In the seaweed groves of the temperate North Pacific Ocean grow canopies of great kelps, some of which, like the giant bladder kelp *(Macrocystis),* are 150 feet long. (Marine botanist E. Yale Dawson, whose life was eventually claimed by the ocean in which he had found his career, wrote of the giant bladder kelp that its "growth in length is the fastest in the plant kingdom and exceeds that of fast-growing tropical bamboos." Groves of this kelp along the California coast are as productive per square meter as are sugarcane fields under intensive cultivation in Java.) Below the stalks of the great kelps grow shorter plants, which form a ground cover or understory, and below these, a turf of velvety species.

Starting with basic green — the color of the chlorophyll pigment essential to all photosynthetic plants — nature has endowed the seaweeds with other pigments, which in combination with green, produce overall hues of crimson, purple, olive, or brown. The nongreen pigments act partly as filters to screen out the wavelengths of light that are useless to the plants.

Kelp (Nereocystis) *draped over driftwood by falling tide, Cypress Island, Washington*

Brown Egregia *and bright-green* Ulva, *Olympic seacoast, Washington*

The adaptive, or survival, value of most seaweed structures is plain enough. Many species have gas bladders that keep their fronds floating in the upper sunlit waters. In the kelps, an interlacing claw holdfast at the base of the stalk anchors the plant to its rocky bed. The slime exuded by all seaweeds protects them from abrasion and keeps them from drying when they are exposed to the air at low tide.

Among the seaweeds there are few structural counterparts of the thorns and poisons that protect land plants from grazing animals. (Indeed, on the Orkney Islands of Scotland, seaweeds provide the year-round diet of primitive breeds of sheep!) The tissues of the rock algae and coralline algae, worldwide in distribution, are harsh and limy. Some species of

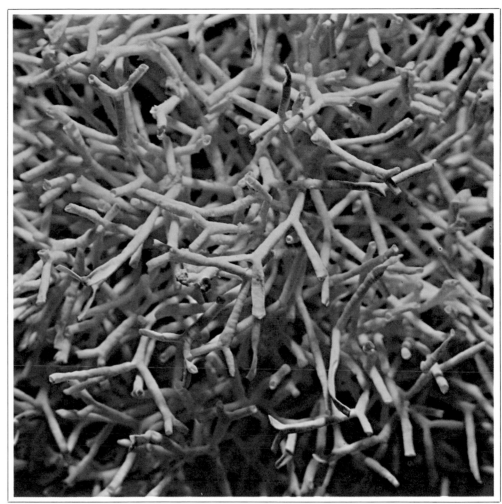

Tiny white calcareous alga, Amphiroa fragilissima, *Grand Cayman Island, British West Indies*

Caulerpa, tropical green seaweeds of feathery or fernlike shape, contain chemicals that are mildly poisonous to man. We may ask why, during the evolution of the marine plants, did not more species acquire structures repellent to vegetarian fishes, sea urchins, snails, and crabs?

Plant Repatriates to the Sea

A few flowering plants return to the salty margins of the mother sea

Mainly green surfgrass, Phyllospadix scouleri, and brown feather boa (Egregia), west coast of Whidbey Island, Washington

About four hundred million years ago the first land vegetation emerged from tropical marine estuaries and began to blanket the earth with green. About two hundred million years ago the descendants of the primitive land plants became the first flowering plants. Still later, some few of the flowering plants returned to the salty margins of the mother sea. These repatriates now live in three zones that parallel the tide line.

Living in shallow waters are the sea grasses, such as eelgrass and surfgrass, whose emerald ribbons are familiar to beachcombers. The sea grasses of the North Pacific are fed upon with relish by brant, widgeon, and other waterfowl. In southern seas, beds of turtle grass, manatee grass, and dugong grass furnish food to the marine animals that lend their names to those plants. Endless tropical coasts are lined with thickets of the red mangrove tree, which dangles its naked roots in the sea and drops its spearlike fruits into the tidal mud.

Living in the salt marsh zone, and often flooded by high tides, are forms like the pickleweed, with fat succulent leaves and salty sap, and the salt grass, with harsh, stickery leaves.

Farther inland in the spray zone live many species of salt-tolerant forbs, shrubs, and trees. Here you see the blazing reds of the sea grape, the pinky lavenders of the beach morning glory, and the clear yellows of the cinquefoil.

Scattered along many Caribbean shores are little shrubs shaped like Japanese bonsai. The species, known locally as "cuabilla de costa" or saltwater bush, endures incredible extremes of moisture, heat, and salinity. It is fed upon in full, hot sunlight by a marine snail, the beaded periwinkle, which will crawl thirty feet above the beach to find it.

None of the cone-bearing plants (gymnosperms), ferns, or mosses have returned to the sea or to its briny shores. The difficulty of transporting water in their vascular systems and the difficulty of scattering their seeds or spores have perhaps bound them to the land.

Red mangrove, Rhizophora mangle, *sprouting in salt water,*
Grand Cayman Island, British West Indies

Beach morning glory, Ipomea pes-caprae, *on limerock shore,*
Grand Cayman Island, British West Indies

Cinquefoil, five finger (Potentilla),
St. Paul Island, Alaska

Some species of lichens do, however, flourish on rocks in the spray zone. These hardy plants — each one a fungus wedded to an alga — have great powers of survival, not only on the shores but in hot springs, in deserts, and in arctic-alpine regions beyond the endurance limits of other plants.

It cannot be said that the seashore plants "choose" to live where they do. They are simply winners within the plant kingdom of a perennial struggle for existence. They have persevered genetically in a salty environment, which is poisonous to most other species of plants. They are the survivors in a process that is called, in biological shorthand, "competition."

53

Red leaves of sea grape, Coccolaba uvifera, *Grand Cayman Island, British West Indies*

Strategies of Marine Animals

Nature must now be approaching the limits of invention

Edible mussels, Mytilus edulis, *Cape Johnson, Washington*

Snails (Littorina) on rocks at low tide, St. Paul Island, Alaska

Many adaptations — many architectural plans for survival — are displayed by the animals that live in the busy zone where the sea pours endlessly across the sand. Their basic needs are the same as the needs of humans — that is, for food, for shelter from the elements, and for protection from predators or "enemies." Their individual strategies for filling those needs are so manifold as to suggest that Nature must now surely be approaching the limits of invention.

The common blue mussel clings to its rocky bed by means of a waterproof glue, the nature of which continues to baffle industrial chemists. Thousands of tiny whips (cilia) on the gills of the mussel circulate seawater through its body in one direction at the rate of about a quart an hour. Small plankton organisms, mainly bacteria, stick to the gills and are whipped into the mouth as food.

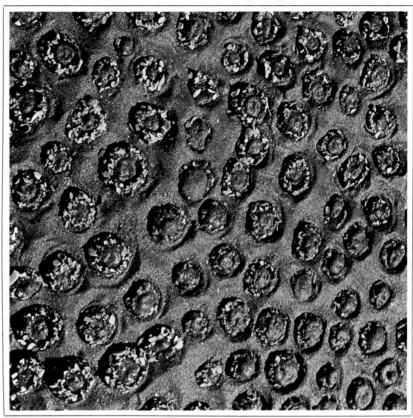

Colonial sea anemones,
Anthopleura elegantissima, *Oregon coast*

Blue crab, Callinectes sapidus, *male,*
Grand Cayman Island, British West Indies

Barnacles compete with mussels for a living. Though a barnacle looks like a mollusk, it is really a crablike crustacean that lives within a limy shell of its own making. Anatomically, it can be said to stand on its head and kick its food into its mouth with its feet.

The green sea anemone feeds upon coarse plankton organisms and upon small fishes and shellfishes that approach within reach of its stinging tentacles. Anemones narcotize their prey by injecting a poison from little sacs in the tentacles. The same poison is produced by certain jellyfish relatives of the anemone and can bring intense pain to a human diver.

Black sea urchin, Diadema antillarum, *Grand Cayman Island, British West Indies*

Snails and sea urchins move slowly over the sea floor or climb into thickets of kelp, grazing with toothlike mouth parts upon many kinds of living and dead organisms. Biologists who are studying the ecology of California kelps — the source of a multimillion-dollar industry — are trying to estimate the grazing impact of snails and sea urchins upon kelp production. And they are trying to estimate the predatory impact of sea otters upon the snails and urchins that eat the kelps. Life relations along the shore are indeed complex and mysterious.

Of all the myriad scavengers of the shore, crabs are the most diverse in form and habit. Some crawl, some swim, some burrow in the mud, some hide in the shells of mollusks, and some have left the sea behind (except at breeding time) to wander over land and even to climb trees. Some still resemble things that crawled when the world was new.

Preyed upon by fishes, sea birds, sea otters, seals, and porpoises, some crabs adopt camouflage for protection; they deliberately dress their shells with bits of seaweed chosen to blend with the habitat. In others — the hermit crabs — the rear end of the body has become spiral in shape, enabling the animal to screw itself into an empty snail shell. As it grows in size it must periodically dash from its outgrown shell to a roomier one.

Every seashore animal protects itself from predators by some device, such as a hard shell, a coat of thorny spines or stinging darts, or simply a concealing habit. Anyone who has trod barefoot on a sea urchin will

Sabellid worms (Eudistylia) *withdrawn into their tubes at low tide, Whidbey Island, Washington*

agree. Even the naked sea slug, which is often seen gliding across intertidal grass beds of our warmer coasts, and which seems to be quite unprotected, will, if disturbed, emit a cloud of purple ink to confound an intruder.

The shells of most sea snails are coiled in a right-handed spiral; those of a few, left-handed. But why — or perhaps why not?

Animal Repatriates to the Sea *Shaped for life in the sea and on the shore*

Steller's sea lions, Eumetopias jubatus, *and cormorants* (Phalacrocorax), *near Florence, Oregon*

Within the animal kingdom are several hundred vertebrate, air-breathing species — the marine reptiles, birds, and mammals — whose earliest ancestors lived in the sea, whose later ancestors invaded the continents, and whose still later ancestors turned back to the ocean. The modern repatriates have advanced in a circle.

Some of the repatriates persist in returning to the land (or to rafts of ice) each year at breeding time. About one quarter of the sea snakes and all of the sea lizards, sea turtles, sea birds, seals, and sea otters crawl out of the water in order to lay eggs or to give birth. The remaining sea snakes, and all of the whales, porpoises, manatees, and dugongs, give birth in the water to live babies, which had earlier hatched within the mother's body.

Amphibians, the first vertebrates to leave the sea, have not really returned. None is truly marine, though a few are tolerant of brackish or full-strength seawater. The crab-eating frog of the Gulf of Thailand, for example, swims among the mangroves at high tide in search of food.

Of the many animal stocks that tried to make the passage from land to sea, some failed. We know of their ventures only from the fossil record. Such a one was *Archaeopteryx,* a pigeon-sized shorebird having claws on its wings and teeth in its jaws, known from Jurassic slates one hundred forty million years old. Another was *Kolponomos,* a kind of seagoing raccoon the size of a bear, whose remains are known from marine sediments of Washington and Oregon.

While the primitive marine air-breathers were adapting to aquatic life, they were slowly being shaped in form and function to meet four challenges of the sea. The sea is cold, fluid, three-dimensional, and salty. In combination, these represent barriers to any continental vertebrate that "chooses" to leave the sheltered land for the open shore, or for the deep sea beyond it.

Resting California sea lions, mostly adult males, Año Nuevo Island, California

Modern sea snakes, including about fifty kinds in the tropical Indian and Pacific Oceans, have flat bodies, which impart speed in swimming. The nostrils are on top of the head and can be closed by valves when the snake dives. Special glands in the head dispose of sea salt accidentally swallowed. The bite of all sea snakes is poisonous.

Of the few lizards that are truly marine, the most striking is the big, sociable iguana of the Galapagos Islands. It will dive thirty-five feet or more and remain underwater for fifty minutes. A few crocodile species are marine, though most live in fresh water.

Five species of turtles have returned to the sea. All have paddle feet (flippers), all are migratory, and all lay their eggs on sandy beaches. The famous annual journey of the green turtle from the coastal waters of Brazil to Ascension Island, a dot on the map of the South Atlantic Ocean, covers fourteen hundred miles. The migration route is still mysterious. How did it evolve? How do the turtles set a true course for their tiny island? Where do the young ones disappear after hatching? Where in the ocean are their hidden nurseries?

Soon after the first birds evolved, some species began to exploit the food riches of the shore. Their descendants, now called the shorebirds, number about three hundred species and include the sandpipers, gulls, auks, puffins, and others.

Among them are the strongest fliers. The golden plover migrates twenty-four hundred miles nonstop with only a two-ounce weight loss. Sooty terns swirl by the millions above tropical seas; they fly continually without rest for months on end. Flocks of little sanderlings along the Washington coast seem to play tag with the waves. They lift in alarm and change course in unison as though directed by a single mind.

The amphibious carnivores — the round-eyed seals, sea lions, and walruses — are beasts of compromise. Down through the ages they have been shaped for life both in the sea and on the shore (or on ice). They must keep warm underwater and yet not overheat in sunlight. They must be equipped to swim and yet to walk or wriggle on the solid substrates where they breed. The newborn pups must be large enough to survive exposure to weather at birth and yet not so large as to endanger the life of the mother during parturition.

Coastal animals, trapped by geography in their narrow worlds, are easy victims of man. The Steller's sea cows, which lived in the kelps of the North Pacific rim from California to Japan, were first decimated by

Thick-billed murres, black-legged kittiwakes, and red-legged kittiwakes,
St. Paul Island, Alaska

prehistoric hunters and then exterminated by eighteenth-century
European adventurers. Today, their living relatives, the manatees and
dugongs, are in trouble almost everywhere throughout their ranges. The
last Caribbean monk seals and Japanese sea lions were killed in the
1940s. Many local breeding stocks of sea turtles and crocodiles have
disappeared, while others are endangered.

Shores Forever

Trust them for their naturalness and love them for their power to move us

Receding tide, Netarts Bay, Oregon

In the foregoing essays I have tried to translate certain messages that flow from the shore. I have touched fleetingly on that narrow zone between land and sea to which men turn in search of the wellsprings of art, of the clearest evidence of geologic change, of the oldest plant and animal genealogies, and of the greatest diversity of life on earth.

I hope that our children in school will be taught that the shorelines are priceless records of prehistoric events. The beaches are part of all they have met for fifty million centuries. One can find there, preserved in fossil corals and shells, growth lines indicating that the earth's rotation is slowing down — that the days are getting longer. The decline was predicted by observers of the moon's tidal drag and was later proved by the skeletons of creatures long buried in the rocks.

From the time of the ancient astronomers down to the present, scholars have compared the length of the tidal, or lunar, month (29.3 days) with that of the estral month in women (28.3 days). The correlation may be false or it may indeed show that the rhythm of Mesozoic tides continues to beat in the bloodstream of humankind.

Pebbles and boulders strewn along polar and temperate shores tell tales of the coming and going of ice ages. As the massive continental glaciers moved downward and seaward, they ripped off native rocks and carried them hundreds of miles. Granite, sandstone, basalt, felsite, pumice, quartz, agate, jasper, and many other rocks and minerals now lie bare on the shores, far from their points of origin.

The shores are continuous garden strips where fertilizing elements brought down by rivers mingle with elements raised to the surface by currents of the continental shelves. They are ancient proving grounds for organisms — Gardens before Eden. Here the limpet learned to wander at night in search of food, and to return at dawn to the exact rock that had served as a template for its growing shell. Here a hundred thousand different kinds of plants and animals are held by ligaments of habit and adaptation.

Pebbles, selected for their beauty from beaches, Puget Sound, Washington

It will be proof of our own ability to survive as a species if we learn to respect the wild, clean shores of the world; to trust them for their naturalness and to love them for their power to move us.

Their beauty must not be sold. I believe that we will increasingly question the morality and legality of individual property "rights" to shores. The right to own is near the right to damage. Christopher Stone, professor of law, believes that shores have a reasonable right to "protest" when they are harmed. In the *Southern California Law Review* in 1972, he wrote, "I favor a system in which the [legal guardian, or trustee, or conservator] would urge before the court injuries not presently cognizable — the death of eagles and inedible crabs, the suffering of sea lions, the loss from the face of the earth of species of commercially valueless birds, the disappearance of a wilderness area."

The margins of the World Ocean are a common good reserved to no one generation in its time. The preservation of shorelines and beaches calls for a basic decency not unlike the ethics that have led men and women in the past to save religions, art treasures, historical landmarks, and poems. It calls for the steady concern and the directed labor of those who belong (as E.M. Forster might put it) to an "aristocracy of the sensitive." In the reality and wholeness of shores, and not in their potentials for "development" or "production," remain their everlasting wealth.

Channeled mudflats at low tide, Willapa Bay, Washington

Can we preserve the earthly sources of our humanity or can we not? If we elect to scar, mine, and poison these sources, we will surely bring to each the end of a history far older and more complete than our own.

73

Action for Conservation

Our natural shores will stand a better chance of surviving, I think, if we talk more about their beauty, meaning, and importance and less about how rottenly we are treating them. I do not suggest that we wholly abandon outrage against shore contamination by chemicals, oil spills, pathogens, and garbage, and against shore destruction by needless engineering works. But talking about only what we are against can be tiresome and, in the long run, unhelpful.

Philosophy aside, what action do I suggest? Simply that as individuals we join, or contribute to, groups concerned with saving wild lands and dedicating them for nondestructive use. This is the least we can do.

My own favorite group is the Nature Conservancy (founded in 1946) which has saved over one million acres of land and water in the United States for the use of educators, naturalists, hikers, and boaters. (This and several hundred other groups, are described in the *Conservation Directory,* published annually by the National Wildlife Federation, 1412 16th Street Northwest, Washington, D.C. 20036.)

The Wilderness Society (1935) is among the leading groups that emphasize the spiritual values of relict American wilderness. The American Littoral Society (1961) fosters public interest in marine and estuarine natural history.

The Environmental Defense Fund (1967) and the Natural Resources Defense Council (1969) take court action in the interests of society when seacoasts and other wild places are threatened. Legal action is often the *only* way to stop shoreline damage.

One of the interests of the International Union for the Conservation of Nature and Natural Resources (IUCN, 1948) is the creation of marine preserves. Mona I. Björklund, ecologist at IUCN headquarters in Switzerland, has published a list of several hundred marine parks of the world *(Environmental Conservation,* 1:205-223, 1974). She lists them either as "primarily marine" or as "coastal with marine component." Fort Jefferson National Monument, Florida, created in 1935, was the first marine area on the North American continent to be given park status.

G. Carleton Ray, zoologist at Johns Hopkins University, has prepared under contract from the IUCN a preliminary classification of coastal and marine environments of the world *(IUCN Occasional Paper* no. 14, 1975). It is a step toward the identification and preservation of critical habitats. It employs a three-part classification — by zoogeographic regions (e.g., American Pacific), by coastal biotic provinces (e.g., Columbian), and by habitats (e.g., exposed rocky coast). And in Tokyo in May, 1975, men and women from thirty-three nations met to talk about methods for establishing marine parks and reserves *(IUCN Publications New Series* no. 37, 1976).

When Daniel B. Beard in 1959 was superintendent of Olympic National Park in the state of Washington he complained that conservation seems to stop at the water's edge. "Parks and reservations usually end right where the amazing biological phenomena of the marine littoral begin. In parks where you would be arrested for picking flowers you can step off into the intertidal zone and take all the sea urchins, starfish, and other things you want."

He spoke in the early dawn of the Age of Environmental Awareness. Protection of shore life has improved since then. Witness the legal arrangements in Washington State where shore management has long been studied. Now Olympic National Park has contractual agreements with three state agencies — the Parks and Recreation Commission, the Game Department, and the Fisheries Department — for protection of those organisms that live below mean high tide line, or the line that marks the lower limit of National Park jurisdiction.

Everywhere in the marine waters of Washington, the Department of Fisheries has authority to regulate the taking of food fish and food shellfish, though not of other shore organisms. If, however, a "recognized substantial use of a species for food" develops, the department can classify it as food and can begin to regulate its taking. (Witness the recent market for sea urchins.) The department should perhaps have authority to manage *all* shore organisms for their multiple use in recreation, education, and research, as well as in commerce.

Under the innovative Coastal Zone Management Act of 1972, the federal government has been helping the coastal states plan for orderly use of shores. In 1976, Washington became the first state to receive a federal grant ($2 million), thanks to the fact that Washingtonians had already adopted by referendum in November 1972 a "mini-CZM" program.

Further Reading

The level of reading difficulty for each book is shown by the letter **N** for nonspecialist, **C** for college graduate, or **P** for professional.

Unfortunately, I do not have space to list inspirational books. For examples, look in your local library under the names of Henry Beston, Ernest Braun, Rachel Carson, Douglas Faulkner, John Hay, Don Greame Kelley, Carlton Ogburn, and Stella Snead.

Abbott, Tucker R. *American Seashells: The Marine Mollusca of the Atlantic and Pacific Coasts of North America.* New York: Van Nostrand-Reinhold, 1974. A large book covering 6,409 species of mollusks, most of them described and illustrated by drawings or photos. Includes 35 references. **C**

Carefoot, Thomas H. *Pacific Seashores: A Guide to Seashore Ecology.* Seattle and Vancouver, B.C.: University of Washington Press and J.J. Douglas, 1977. The author is a zoology professor at the University of British Columbia. **N**

Carr, Archie. *The Reptiles.* New York: Time-Life Books (Life Nature Library), 1963. A masterful writer tells how certain land snakes, lizards, crocodilians, and turtles have adapted to life in salt water. Includes 60 references. **N**

Clark, John. *Coastal Ecosystem Management: A Technical Manual for the Conservation of Coastal Zone Resources.* New York: John Wiley and Sons for the Conservation Foundation (Washington, D.C.), 1977. A 4-pound book dealing with biological, technological, and administrative aspects of shore management. It may well be, as the jacket states, "the only complete text available" in its field. **P**

Flora, Charles J., and Fairbanks, Eugene. *The Sound and the Sea: A Guide to Northwestern Neritic Invertebrate Zoology.* 3d ed. Olympia: Washington State Department of Printing, 1977. A pictorial guide that is crammed with keys and photos for more than 300 species (usually one species to a page) and includes some comments on their biology. **N** and **C**

Green, James. *The Biology of Estuarine Animals.* Seattle: University of Washington Press, 1975. Corollary reading for college students. Includes information about habitats, communities, and populations of estuarine animals from plankton to birds. **C**

Hart, John Lawson. *Pacific Fishes of Canada.* Ottawa: Fisheries Research Board of Canada, Bulletin 180, 1973. A comprehensive book on Pacific Northwest saltwater fishes. Includes a history of local ichthyology and oceanography, species accounts (description, range, life history, and importance to man), gazeteer of place names, glossary, and about 900 references (a 4-pound treasure at $14.40). **P**

Hewlett, Stefani, and K. Gilbey Hewlett. *Sea Life of the Pacific Northwest*. Toronto: McGraw-Hill / Ryerson, 1976. The authors are curators in Vancouver, B.C., Public Aquarium, as well as teachers and tour leaders. Over 200 photos and a lively, fact-filled text cover inshore organisms from seaweeds to fishes and whales (no birds). 47-item bibliography and large format. **N**

Kirk, Ruth. *The Olympic Seashore*. 6th printing, Port Angeles, Wash.: Olympic Natural History Association in cooperation with the National Park Service, 1974. Might be entitled "How to Enjoy the Olympic Beaches." Provides general coverage and 6 maps and charts of interesting beaches (a bargain at $1.95). **N**

Kozloff, Eugene N. *Seashore Life of Puget Sound, the Strait of Georgia, and the San Juan Archipelago*. 2d printing, with corrections, of the 1973 ed. Seattle: University of Washington Press, 1974. A guide to identification and natural history of the intertidal seaweeds and invertebrates of the Pacific Northwest. **C**

Lane, Frank W. *Kingdom of the Octopus: The Life History of the Cephalopoda*. New York: Sheridan House, 1960. A richly anecdotal account of the molluscan class that includes octopus, cuttlefish, and squid. 16 full-color plates, 95 black-and-white photos and drawings, and scientific appendices. **N**

Nehls, Harry B. *Familiar Birds of Northwest Shores and Waters*. Portland, Oreg.: Portland Audubon Society, 1975. A slick-paper, pocket-size guide to Pacific Northwest waterfowl, and the bald eagle and osprey. 100 species illustrated by color paintings. **N**

Ricketts, Edward F., and Calvin, Jack. *Between Pacific Tides*. 4th ed., rev. Joel W. Hedgpeth. Stanford, Calif.: Stanford University Press, 1968. Detailed descriptions of habitats and species. An 80-page "systematic index" combines a list of organisms from plants to mammals with references to literature about them. **C**

Scheffer, Victor B. *A Natural History of Marine Mammals*. New York: Charles Scribner's Sons, 1976. The adaptations of 111 species of mammals to life in the sea. Includes 39 references and a chart showing the origins of sea otters, walking seals, crawling seals, sirenians, toothed cetaceans, and baleen cetaceans. **N**

Smith, Lynwood S. *Living Shores of the Pacific Northwest*. Seattle: Pacific Search Press, 1976. A lucid guide to the "complexities and beauties of the seashore environment, with a minimum of technical terminology." 148 photos (110 color) of species and habitats are grouped according to site (rocky, gravel, sandy, or mud beach; or floats). Maps and location guides to beaches of British Columbia, Washington, and Oregon. Written by a professor of fisheries at the University of Washington. **N**

Somerton, David, and Murray, Craig. *Field Guide to the Fish of Puget Sound and the Northwest Coast.* Seattle: Washington Sea Grant Program, distributed by University of Washington Press, 1976. Designed to help divers, anglers, and tide pool explorers identify 99 inshore fishes. For each species, there is an ink drawing and a brief description. Printed on water-resistant stock in a paperback format. **N**

Vancouver Natural History Society. *Nature West Coast: A Study of Plants, Insects, Birds, Mammals and Marine Life as seen in Lighthouse Park.* Vancouver, B.C.: Discovery Press, 1973. A charming in-depth biological survey of a 185-acre peninsula near Vancouver. **N**

Waaland, Robert J. *Common Seaweeds of the Pacific Coast.* Seattle: Pacific Search Press, 1977. Distribution by tidal habitats and by geography, species accounts (35 illustrated in monochrome, 43 in color), uses by man, interactions with inshore animals, and recipes for cooking. College level reading but easy to follow. I endorse the author's use of Latin names for organisms that neither have, nor deserve to have, vernacular names. **C**

Wahl, Terence R., and Paulson, Dennis R. *A Guide to Bird Finding in Washington.* 2d ed. Bellingham, Wash.: Whatcom Museum Press, 1974. This useful booklet lists all the birds of Washington and British Columbia according to habitat (e.g., rocky shore, sandy shore, mud flat, and salt marsh) and abundance. It tells you how to reach birding places and assumes that you will know what you are looking at once you get there. **N**

Williams, Richard L. *The Northwest Coast.* New York: Time-Life Books (The American Wilderness Series), 1973. A richly illustrated account of shores and adjacent regions. See also, in the same series, *Atlantic Beaches* by Jonathan Norton Leonard, 1972, and *The Northeast Coast* by Maitland E. Edey, 1972. **N**

Other Books from Pacific Search Press

COOKING

Asparagus: The Sparrowgrass Cookbook by Autumn Stanley. Over 100 ways to serve the low-calorie, nutritious vegetable of kings. Includes helpful tips on cultivation. Drawings. 160 pp. $3.95.

Bone Appétit! Natural Foods for Pets by Frances Sheridan Goulart. Treat your pet to some home-cooked meals made only with pure, natural ingredients. Recipes fit for both man and beast! Drawings. 96 pp. $2.95.

The Carrot Cookbook by Ann Saling. Over 200 mouth-watering recipes. Drawings. 160 pp. $3.50.

The Crawfish Cookbook by Norma S. Upson. Try the lobster's freshwater cousin, the crayfish, for inexpensive gourmet dining. Over 100 recipes for every time of day. Drawings. 160 pp. $3.95.

The Dogfish Cookbook by Russ Mohney. Over 65 piscine delights. Cartoons and drawings. 108 pp. $1.95.

The Green Tomato Cookbook by Paula Simmons. More than 80 solutions to the bumper crop. 96 pp. $2.95.

Wild Mushroom Recipes by the Puget Sound Mycological Society. 2d edition. Over 200 recipes. 176 pp. $6.95.

The Zucchini Cookbook by Paula Simmons. Revised and enlarged 2d edition. Over 150 tasty creations. 160 pp. $3.50.

CRAFT

Spinning and Weaving with Wool by Paula Simmons. Over 20 years of experience enables the author to give you all the essentials for becoming a successful spinner and weaver of handspun wool. 162 black-and-white photographs, 76 technical drawings, 33 line drawings. 224 pp. $9.95; cloth, $17.95.

NATURE

Butterflies Afield in the Pacific Northwest by William Neill / Douglas Hepburn, photography. Lovely guide with 74 unusual color photos of living butterflies. 96 pp. $5.95.

Cascade Companion by Susan Schwartz / Bob and Ira Spring, photography. Nature and history of the Washington Cascades. Black-and-white photos, maps. 160 pp. $5.95.

Common Seaweeds of the Pacific Coast by J. Robert Waaland. Introduction to the seaweed world — its biology, conservation, and many uses for both industry and seafood lovers. 42 color photos; diagrams, illustrations. 136 pp. $5.95.

Fire and Ice: The Cascade Volcanoes by Stephen L. Harris. Copublished with the Mountaineers. Black-and-white photos, drawings, maps. 320 pp. $7.95.

Little Mammals of the Pacific Northwest by Ellen Kritzman. The only book devoted solely to the Northwest's little mammals. 48 color and black-and-white photos; distribution maps, index. 128 pp. $5.95.

Living Shores of the Pacific Northwest by Lynwood Smith / Bernard Nist, photography. Fascinating guide to seashore life. Over 140 photos, 110 in color. 160 pp. $9.95.

Minnie Rose Lovgreen's Recipe for Raising Chickens by Minnie Rose Lovgreen. 2d edition. 32 pp. $2.00.

Sleek & Savage: North America's Weasel Family by Delphine Haley. Extraordinary color and black-and-white photos; bibliography. 128 pp. $5.50.

Why Wild Edibles? The Joys of Finding, Fixing, and Tasting — West of the Rockies by Russ Mohney. Color and black-and-white photos, illustrations. 320 pp. $6.95.